MEI LAN-FANG IN "THE BANDIT GENERAL"

*Studies in*

# THE CHINESE DRAMA

By KATE BUSS

*New York*
*Jonathan Cape & Harrison Smith*

PRINTED IN THE UNITED STATES BY
THE VAIL-BALLOU PRESS AND BOUND
BY THE J. F. TAPLEY CO.

*"Without error there could be no such thing as truth."*
CHINESE PROVERB

# Contents

# *Illustrations*

# *Introduction*

ARTS may emerge as absurdities after revolutions. Except as history the classical drama in China might have ended with the dissolution of the empire nearly twenty years ago. But the tradition that had maintained it as a popular art during the previous six centuries continues it as the popular theatre of today in China. Deviations in occasional small playhouses are said to be uninteresting and without influence.

This book is concerned with the classical drama. Its objective is to assemble facts rather than to be analytical. If legend has entered it as fact this is because legend in China may be so old that it is said to become fact. Very little has been published even in China upon the subject of its theatre. This compilation of text and illustration has been made easier by the assistance of Dr. John Ferguson, Professor Edward S. Morse, Mr. Mei Lan-fang, Mr. Shen Hung and Mr. Aram Antranikian.

The Chinese classical drama has contributed something to the Elizabethan and to the Greek stage.

11

But its immediate attraction for strangers is the amazing beauty with which it presents the contemporary and the traditional life of an opulent and exotic people. Once having considered a Chinese play the occidental mind is eager to be told more about the forty centuries of historical, social and spiritual life reflected in this panorama of blended past, present and tomorrow which is the popular Chinese drama. It is so conventionalized that its changes have usually coincided with the changes of dynasties, and yet it feels as mobile as imagination. Today this Chinese drama is one of the most exacting arts of the world.

But to understand is the dilemma! Foreigners in China have gone to the theatre, particularly to the larger playhouses of Peking, heard the 'clangor' of a music that is unfamiliar both in interval and orchestration, listened to a strange language emerging, often in falsetto, from grotesquely painted faces, observed a magnificence of costumery and an absence of scenery, and, as an unimaginative man lost in a rich wilderness, have recounted a lot of misleading nonsense.

Unlike her Nipponese neighbour, China is not a borrowing nation. And is the harder to understand for it. Her arts of painting, of calligraphy and of literature, as her art of the classical drama, are indigenous, and can be received in their magnificence only when disassociated from opposing traditions, from the fine arts of other nations. Chinese classical drama is so completely an entity that it is comparable only to its own evolving perfection . . . but why attempt a comparison of the incomparable?

KATE BUSS

NEW YORK
March, 1930

THE GREAT MONAD

I

# *Origin of the Chinese Drama*

THE birth year of the Chinese drama is unknown. Dates are variously suggested and
disagreed upon and enclose a period of
more than twenty-five centuries. The reason for this
divergence of opinion is that while one writer considers the pantomimic dances—for religious worship
or military jubilation—which were presented to musical accompaniment, a dramatic production, another
waits to name the century of the initial stage performance until festival rites unite with speech in
dramatic situation and an histrionic dénouement;
or, one studies drama from the assumption of the
aesthetic, and another, the anthropologist, considers
physical trait and language and primitive custom to
find in the emotional agreement in ceremony and
ritual a dramatic presentation.

Like its other arts a nation's drama is a development and is incepted, as they are, by civic and
national ceremony. It is only the shortlived that is

17

born completely functioning. And the tenacious Chinese drama can have had neither a definitely marked inception nor a conclusion for the early scribe to have noted, even in a country of remarkable literary antiquity and the habit of notation. From the cult of the dead Chinese drama has been developed by assimilation, by the patronage of succeeding emperors, and the corresponding conversion of the Chinese people.

Historians say that music existed in China in B. C. 5400. Of China's second dynasty and its "Golden Age" B. C. 2205–1766, we read that religious worship was accompanied by music and dances which represented the occupations of the people—plowing and harvesting, war and peace; and that these dances illustrated the sensations of working, joy, fatigue, and content.

The Chou Ritual classic written several centuries before the time of Confucius states that six ceremonial dances were in vogue at that early period: "In the first, wands with whole feathers were waved—in the worship of the spirits of agriculture; in the second wands with divided feathers were used—in the ancestral temples; in the third feather caps were worn on the head, and the upper garments were adorned with kingfisher feathers—in blessing the four quarters of the realm; in the fourth yak-tails were used—in ceremonial for the promotion of harmony; in the fifth shields were manipulated—to celebrate military merit; in the sixth the bare hands were waved—in homage to the stars and constellations.

But the ceremonial dances chiefly in vogue were to celebrate, and partly to portray, civil and military accomplishment. "Royal music was of two kinds. If civil merit was to be celebrated the posturers grasped feather wands; if martial prowess, they grasped vermilion shields and jade (embossed) battle-axes. The jade signified virtue, and the shields benevolence, to inculcate clemency to those defeated." [1]

Here, without question, is action to an accompaniment of music. Speech and song were a later emanation. Gradually these dances expressed more license than litany and during the Chou dynasty, B. C. 1122-255, were forbidden in association with religious worship; they were then presented under separate ceremonials but continued to give honour to the same symbols. Elaborate and fantastic costumery and an increased ballet were added and pantomime had become a spectacle for popular entertainment, and was presented on a stage built for the purpose instead of in a temple.

[1] W. Arthur Cornaby in "The New China Review" for March, 1919.

Other early Chinese writers mention occurrences which establish the fact of some form of drama: we read of an emperor who lived seventeen hundred years before the Christian era who was commended for having forbidden certain stage conventions; another ruler of a pre-Christian dynasty was deprived of funeral honours because he was thought to have too much enjoyed the theatre; and a third emperor was advised to exclude actors from his court.

Emile Guimet [1] says that a Chinese theatre was established by an emperor about B. C. 700 and that the writers of that century applied themselves to the development of a poetic drama. Any literature which may have existed has been destroyed by succeeding rulers.

We find more definite drama chronicle of the eighth century. The emperor Hsuan Tsung, or Ming Huang as he is commonly called from a posthumous title, established a school in the gardens of his palace to teach young men and women the arts of dancing and music, and probably chose his court entertainers from this group. Many actors of today associate themselves with this early imperial school and call themselves members of the College of the Pear Orchard. Ming Huang, who is said to have acted upon his own stage, is today's patron saint of all actors,

[1] "Théatre Chinois."

and his statue, with incense burning before it, may be seen in Chinese greenrooms.

Plays during this century, which is sometimes called the first period of Chinese drama, focused on extraordinary themes, and anticipated the present heroic drama. It is probable that interest in the drama did not extend further than the Imperial court until the thirteenth century.

During the Yüan dynasty, founded in 1280 by the Mongol warrior Kublai Khan, drama, as it now exists in China, appears to have slipped into being as quietly as a fall of snow overnight, and as far as most historians are concerned with the subject, is an established fact only from this time. What actually happened in the thirteenth century was that divisions of subject and character were fixed and an enduring literature produced.

# II

## *Types of Plays*

VENERATION of the dead controlled China centuries before Confucius wrote "Ever think of your ancestors and cultivate virtue," and is today the active principle in the moral and mental lives of four hundred millions of Chinese. Arts are featured by this national superstition and frequently seem to have endured because of it; the routine of diurnal living and the festival and ceremony of birth and burial proclaim the animate influence of the departed. Someone has said that China is a country where a few hundred millions of living are terrorized by a few thousand millions of dead.

In the drama ancestor worship is an emphasized and recurrent theme.

Of the three types of plays that are said to include all the variations of contemporary dramatic presentation the Vun Pan Shi is known as the oldest form. Patriotism and filial devotion are its subjects; and in

MEI LAN-FANG AS A WARRIOR IN "THE RAINBOW PASS"

it music and action unite to play upon the emotions of the audience.

The Jin Pan Shi presents civil and military conditions. The difference between the Vun Pan Shi and the Jin Pan Shi is not in the libretto as one might suppose, but in the manner of singing certain rôles and in the tradition of the acting.

A third dramatic form is the Vun Min Shi or "modern" play. Colloquial dialects are allowed in the Vun Min Shi instead of Mandarin—the dialect of Peking—which is the accepted speech of the stage as well as of the nation.

Another classification [1] is the Cheng-pan or historical plays; the Chu-tou, civil pieces; and the Ku-wei or farces.

A civil and a military play must be included on each day's program; the latter is a popular subject that may appear in several of the six or eight plays presented during an evening.

Civil and military plays are sometimes mistakenly said to represent comedy and tragedy. Like the Hindu the Chinese stage does not distinguish carefully between the two; and when a so-called tragedy is presented it usually takes the form of melodrama with a "happy" ending. "Beauty" [2] is a rare example

[1] W. Stanton.
[2] Translated by the Reverend J. Macgowan.

of a Chinese stage tragedy. "Beauty" was a faithful Chinese maiden who was lured from her home by wandering marauders; and the story of her patriotism and tragic death is a popular one in Chinese theatres. But the Chinese are instinctively a humorous people—even the lines of their architecture turn up like a smiling mouth—and as entertainment they prefer to laugh than to cry.

Men and women who have conducted themselves heroically while alive and who in a European country might be known as saints or martyrs are deities in China and may appear as characters in the civil plays which are written around domestic incident, and in the military plays of historical and legendary fact.

Military plays are concerned with historical episode and heroic or filial acts. Civil plays, frequently of a farcical nature, deal with the entanglements of every day life.

As they may be read in classical collections Chinese plays—like Chinese poetry—are straightforward in any seeming unmoral tenets they may hold. And, before accepting the statement that the Chinese stage is immoral, the foreigner should recall that plays exist as they are to be read, as they appear in acting editions, and also as they may be interpreted and developed by the actor who is sometimes allowed great license in "gagging." In most reputable theatres plays teach the wisdom of morality; and indeed the dénouement of a comedy is usually the triumph of virtue over the machinations of some evil influence.

The Chinese penal code states the aim of dramatic performances to be to offer either real or imagined pictures of just and honourable men, chaste women, and obedient children who will encourage the spectator in the practice of virtue. The writer of an indecent play is supposed—even after death—to be persecuted by evil spirits as long as his play appears upon any stage.

China has no stage censor. Anyone may set up a theatre, elaborate his artistic principles or develop his business theories without fear of the hectoring thumb; and, except for the rule which was enforced during the imperialistic government forbidding the impersonation of a reigning emperor, any spectacle and any type of character may be presented.

Plots are usually simple and well sustained but subjects are numerous and of wide range. While the most enduring plays feature the history of the country, others, no less frequently seen, include such subjects as filial and parental piety; the exaltation of learning; native vices and peculiarities of official corruption; vices common to mankind; legal anomalies; and the absurdities of religious practices. The depravity of the priesthood and the corruption of official China have been two controlling elements that are lashed by the dramatist, and as theatre subjects never fail to find appreciative audiences. The five blessings for which the Chinese pray, and which are also libretto subjects, are sons, riches, long life, recovery from sickness, and office. It is noticeable that these are all material blessings . . . even the wish for sons springs from the desire to provide for old age, and as a means to placate the gods after the death of parents. Other favours that the Chinese ask of their gods are that crops shall be well protected and harvests rich, and that men and beasts shall be immune from cholera. To obtain these gifts the people offer the pageants and festivals which have become so popular a form of dramatic presentation in the open fields of the countryside in the spring and autumn. Such spectacles may be financed by the rich man of the village or by a community.

If rains are heavy, prayer and sacrifice are commonly offered to the god of rain that he will close the gates of Heaven in order that the rice will not rot from too profuse a supply of moisture; and to the god of the harvest thanks are returned, in drama festival, for bountiful crops.

Puppet shows are a form of amusement common to many nations and to which certain writers attribute the beginning of the Chinese drama. In some sections of the country a dramatic performance invariably opens with marionettes. Punch and Judy are more frequently seen in the East than in the West and are probably a product of the Chinese imagination.

Confucian themes include the popular cult for learning and filial devotion. Buddhism is the source of most of the buffoonery and farce; in the theatre it not only defies but debases; it makes hideous the actual and enhances the chimerical, and suggests comic relief from religious hysteria. Not all Chinese believe in the divinity of Buddha—or Fu as he is sometimes called—but all men who go to the Chinese theatre know his stage omnipotence.

Satire is always a development of an old civilization and in that ageless country of stability and decay is a style which is profoundly and profusely worked upon. The Chinese understands and responds to satirical comedy. He is directed on the honourable path by its smile and intrigued by its humour. Even when the Chinese dramatist writes about love he handles it with humour—with irony. To the Oriental a love that torments and tyrannizes is an absurd and stupid exaggeration, and the drama that depicts it has small chance of success.

Plays are divided into acts and scenes. Change of

scene is indicated by pantomime, or by a rapid walk
about the stage of all the characters in the piece. Acts
usually number four and the first may be preceded by
a prologue which is spoken by one of the principal
characters. The dénouement occurs in the final act.
Dualism of contrasted scene with scene achieves the
dramatic effect as in Western theatres.

# III

# The Plays as Literature

ALTHOUGH nearly all Chinese plays in contemporary use date from one of the three prolific literary periods of the country it is agreed they lack the literary value of the poetry and the novels written during the same epochs. The Tang dynasty, A. D. 720–905; the Sung dynasty, A. D. 969–1277; and the Yüan dynasty established in 1277 and defeated by the native Chinese in 1368—of which the third is the most important—are the significant periods both of general literature and of the drama, and provide the theatre of today with the great bulk of its plays. Contemporary drama writing usually follows the Mongol (Yüan) construction.

Five hundred plays of known authorship are ascribed to the Yüan dynasty. Among the eighty-five names of playwrights Bazin mentions four women, Tchao-Ming-king, Tchang-koue-pin, Hong-tseu-li-eul, and Hoa-li-lang, each of whom wrote several plays. On the list of men who were dramatists of this same period are Kouan-han-king, the author of sixty dramas; Kao-wen-sieou with thirty to perpetuate his name; Tching-té-hoeü, who wrote eighteen plays; and Pé-jin-fou, fifteen.[1]

"The Romance of the Western Pavilion" is said to be the first play to have been translated into a European language. And as Chinese literature it ranks as one of the best examples; this play was written in the late thirteenth or early fourteenth century, and as "Hsi-siang-chi" is well known to this generation of theatregoers. It is the story of the scholar named Chang who makes love to his hostess' daughter Ying-ling and leaves her in order to compete in the government examinations. This separation by examinations is a frequent theme that is inherited from Confucian precept.

In 1755 a Jesuit priest named Prémare translated in French "Tchao-chi-Kou-eul," or "L'Orphelin de la Chine." In it cruelty and craft are conquered by self-sacrifice, and the play is probably the nearest approach to tragic exposition that any Chinese dramatist has accomplished. When Voltaire adapted this play to the French stage he wrote of it, "Malgré l'incroyable, il y regne de l'interêt et malgré la foule des évenements tout est de la clarté la plus lumineuse." He added that in spite of the fact that it lacked eloquence, reason, and passion it was a more

[1] These titles are in French. In English spelling tch is often written as ch; eu is shortened to u; urh becomes êrh, et cetera, and accents, except the circumflex, are omitted.

MEI LAN-FANG IN "THE RAINBOW PASS"

brilliant play than any that French dramatists had produced during the same period—the fourteenth century. If Voltaire could have read a later translation, made in 1834 by Stanislas Strange, in which the songs are included (a poignant part of any Chinese drama that is too often supposed unimportant because sung) he would have recognized the passion and reason and eloquence that are in the original play.

"Tchao-Mei-Hiang" or "Les Intrigues d'une Soubrette" is a comedy in prose and verse that is translated into French, and offers an opportunity to contrast four styles of writing which follow one another almost on succeeding pages. In scene four of the first act Siao-man speaks in the classic style when she tells her maid, Fan-sou, of Chinese tradition and her own passion for the intellectual life; the speech commences "Du fleuve Ho est sortie la table." The dialogue which follows between Siao-man and Fan-sou is in semi-literary, semi-popular style known in Chinese as pan-wen-pan-sou. In the same scene the verses sung by Fan-sou, who is the principal character and to whom therefore the singing part is given, and which commence "Entendez vous les modulations pures et harmonieuses," are subject to both rhyme and rhythm in the original and are rhythmic in the translation. In the answer that Siao-man makes to

Fan-sou: "Fan-sou, si je consens à aller me promener avec toi, et que Madame Han vienne à le savoir, que deviendrai-je?" the familiar style is used.

Modes of speech usually correspond to types of character and therefore vary throughout any play.

Mandarin is the dialect of most theatres. Local dialects are sometimes heard in village playhouses and in certain popular farces. Although the Peking dialect is the official one a dozen others are heard in various parts of the country, and they differ as a romance language differs from an Anglo-Saxon. If the stage speech of the actor from Peking is not understood by the Chinese from the South, stage action and characters are so prescribed by tradition, and familiar from frequent repetition that plays, even in an unfamiliar dialect, are intelligible to almost any audience.

The adherence in China's theatre curriculum to the traditions of religious and philosophic teaching, and the playwright's reiteration of historical event and personage as dramatic material, operate conjointly as an educational medium in every part of the country to which the drama penetrates. And this semi-standardization—semi because there is always the possible element of the distorting actor or the too imaginative dramatist—has linked dynasties in a more or less factitious pictorial history.

梅蘭芳

MEI LAN-FANG IN "THE PAVILION AT THE ROYAL MONUMENT"

Thus, operating upon one another like a boomerang, the audience is placidly quiescent when confronted with the monotony of tradition and the playwright is content to rearrange the same stories that were the dramatic inheritance of his predecessors, and each has but little interest in the drama as a form of literature. It is true that, like the poet and the novelist, the playwright is concerned with sentiment and ideals and that he handles them with a suppleness that is eloquent; but the beauty which derives from fine cohesion of thought and harmony of words has been, until recently, and in rare cases, considered to be outside the province of the general theatre.

The actor has been so despised that he has not had the association of scholars, and the playwright has suffered for the actor's stigma. He is not classed among the "literati," and if occasionally a literary man is sufficiently interested in a drama form of literature to write a play he publishes it under a nom de plume.

The fact that it has been the custom to hire a playwright by the season to travel with a troupe of actors to write librettos from popular novels or retell an historic episode, gives an idea of what his status has been, and of the difficulty to be overcome before playwriting in China is considered to be a literary profession.

A collected but incomplete dramatic library exists
in fifteen volumes under the title "Shi K'au." Another, of Mongol plays, the "Yuan Ch'u shuan tsa
chi," is in eight volumes. A Chinese edition of the
latter was published in 1615 that includes one hundred dramas and an illustration for each play. Plays
to be read are shorter than the acting version. Acting
editions may be bought in China three for a penny.
They are thin paper covered volumes in uniform size
and varying colours, and resemble the "Farmer's Al-
manac" of New England book tradition. These editions carry a few stage directions; "entrance" and
"exit" are written as "ascend" and "descend," and
"turn the back and say" replaces the "aside" of the
Western theatre.

There are many Chinese plays that are available
for reading in English, French, and German translations. "Tchao-Mei-Hiang" or "Les Intrigues d'une
Soubrette" [1] is one of the rare Chinese love dramas
and is often played. It was written during the Yüan
dynasty. "Hoei-Lan-Ki" or "The Circle of Chalk" [2]
is a drama of high adventure and the vindication of
personal innocence. "Pi-Pa-Ki" or "L'Histoire du
Luth" written by Kao-tong-kia of the Yüan dynasty
is a popular example of the recurrent theme of filial

[1] Translated by M. Bazin aîné.
[2] Translated by Stanislas Julien.

piety. Filial and family devotion are the love inhibitions of the Chinese mind. A father rules over his son as long as the former lives, and retains a certain dominion after death, and a son's acceptance of this traditional subjection is uncomplaining and complying; he waits for his turn to be the head of the family when he will have the much desired sons of his own. Such filial relations of respect and self-sacrifice are more important to the Chinese than sex love and marriage, and are the dramatist's most passional material.

"Sanh Yoer Gi Ts" or "Leaving a Son in a Mulberry Orchard" is the story of a father's sacrifice. The play dates from the Tsur dynasty and is an example of family pride and integrity. "Ho Din Mung" is another popular play. Its story is from the Chou dynasty, B. C. 1122–25. In it the wife of Tsang Ts dies, and the action centres upon a dream in which Tsang Ts sees his wife's coffin split in pieces by an axe. The Chinese understand the significance of dreams in relation to repressed desire and many of their plays were concerned with this theme a long time before dream purport was written about and treated as a new subject in Europe.

"K'ung Dsun Ci" or "Empty City Trap" is an example of the Jin Pan Shi, or military play, and is the story of an episode of the Hur dynasty. An important city of China—so the story goes—was about to be attacked while its soldiery was absent. The Military Advisor opened the city gates, stationed at the entrances what few soldiers he could command, and armed them with brooms and uniformed them as street sweepers. When the enemy approached it heard these "sweepers" singing of the strength of the city, of its great army, and of plans to torture the captured enemy after battle. The enemy was frightened and ran away. The important city in China was saved. As a drama this bit of history is rich in humour and provides a constant entertainment to the Chinese who, as a race, have a keen sense of the ludicrous.

Other plays in French are "Ho Han-Chan" or "La Tunique Confrontée" a drama in four acts written by a woman, Tchang-Koue-Pin; "Ho-Lang-Tan" or "La Chanteuse," author unknown; "Teou Ngo-Youen" or "Le Ressentiment de Teou Ngo," by Kouan-Han-King.[1]

English translations include "Han-Koong-Tsen" or "The Sorrows of Han," an historical play of conditions existing about the beginning of the Christian era; its moral teaches the evil consequence of luxury and supineness in the reigning emperor; "Ho Man San-Peng Tsu Muk Lan's Parting"; "The Golden

---

[1] These three plays were written during the Yüan dynasty and have been translated by M. Bazin ainé.

Leafed Chrysanthemum"; "The Sacrifice of the Soul of Ho Man Sau"; and "Lao-seng-erh" or "An Heir in His Old Age." The last play is a story of domestic life in which an old man is so desirous of a son to perform the obsequies at his tomb that he takes a young wife into his family. Two plays already mentioned under the French translated titles appear in English as "The Orphan of the Chou Family" and "The Intrigues of a Maid."

If, as we are told, they lack any particular literary merit, they are remarkable documents of the inconceivable magnificence of Imperial China, and the faithful and fantastic and isolated mind of the Chinese people.

# IV

# *Religious Influence upon the Drama*

ONE does not begin to understand the Chinese drama without some knowledge of the religious doctrines and the demonolatry of the Chinese people. Not only was the stage incepted by religious rite but it has remained dependent upon Confucianism, Buddhism, and Taoism for theme and character and symbol.

Superstitions inherited from Buddhistic principles frequently denude the stage of mortality and are the playwright's inspiration for extravaganza; he may create a mise en scène in terrestrial immortality and people it with nostalgic gods and provoking genii and find it more absorbing to an audience than the type of play that transpires on an earthly plane and presents the principles of morality that Confucius meditated upon. The playwright may even unite the two—and add a theme from Taoism—in his high

MEDITATION
A BUDDHIST EXERCISE

romance. But when fact and fancy meet and have been mingled in such heterogeneous drama as this even a Chinese is sometimes unable to decide whether a play that turns on the achievements of a general and attendant genii, or of an emperor and certain immortals, is, except for the genii and the immortals, all reality, or except for the general and the emperor, all supposition. Upon such misleading and rich occasion the general may be as foreign to the battle lists as the genii are to the birth registry, for when a Chinese dramatist most clearly limns the unlikely he may the most ardently surround it with every ramification of the actual.

Confucianism is based upon ancestor worship and teaches that the source of morality is in filial piety. Confucianism is so definite a theory of conduct that it cannot be expressed in many symbolic forms such as Buddhism furnishes, but it provides themes for numberless librettos. Buddhism teaches that release from one's present existence is the greatest happiness. Its four "truths" are that life is sorrow; that the chain of reincarnation results from desire; that the only escape is through annihilation of desire; and that the way of escape is through the "eightfold path" of right belief, right resolve, right words, right acts, right life, right effort, right thinking, right meditation. Buddha denied the virtue of caste, ritual, and asceticism as taught by the Hindu sage Guatama, and insisted upon the necessity of pity, kindness, and patience to receive salvation.

The most common form of Buddhist drama is the fantasia or the buffoonery of deity and demon symbols through which Buddha is frequently worshipped.

Taoism teaches that contemplation and reason, avoidance of force, and disregard of mere ceremony, are the means of regeneration. It may be said that Confucianism is based upon morality, Buddhism upon idolatry, and Taoism on superstition; that the one is man-worship, the second image-worship, and the third spirit-worship. Or, in another form, Confucianism deals with the dead past, Buddhism with the changing future, and Taoism with the evils of the present.

However we classify we shall inevitably mix them and be justified by the fact that a Chinese sometimes confuses, and often has some belief in, all three. A Confucian may worship in a Buddhist temple and follow a Taoist ritual.

Two thousand years of peaceful existence in one country of a trilogy of doctrines, and the common meeting ground of the theatre of gods and demons and genii, of teaching and tenet that represent all three, indicate a certain degree of national religious pliancy.

To add to the long list of mythological beings de-

rived from doctrinal sources are the idols of historic
association which have been deified for battle valour
or for civil accomplishment. During the twelfth century Kaing T'ai Kung deified many soldiers, and in
the fourteenth century the first emperor of the Ming
dynasty appointed a great number of city gods. It
was then only a short step from a "Great man to a
little idol" and ultimately to become both a house-
hold and a stage deity. There seems a god for every
occasion and a dozen needs for his favour every day.

In the Imperial Theatre in Pekin there are three
stages, one above the other: the highest is for gods,
the middle space is for mortals, and the lowest plane
receives the slain villain. Heaven above, the earth be-
neath, and the waters under the earth, with all that
these planes may be supposed to control, appear to
figure in dramatic performances, and may even be
shown during a single play.

Such fantastic, and so traditioned an imagination,
and such uncircumscribed deification baffle the "barbarian" and disqualify him to accept a stage performance with a tenth part of the intelligence and, in
the beginning, almost none of the pleasure he will
remark in every Chinese in the audience. But as he
continues to study the Chinese drama he will not
fail to perceive the virtue—and the attendant weak-
nesses—of ancestor worship, of the belief in recur-

rent life, and the earned privileges of another existence, which govern and satisfy the great majority
of the Chinese people.

If it seems strange to find dogma in the theatre,
the fear of evil demons and the respect for, and placa-
tion of, symbols, we have only to recall that doctrines
and drama have developed concurrently. Any attempt
to separate them might destroy the potency of both;
and would certainly rob the Chinese theatre of many
of its most popular characters.

V

# Types and Characters

ALTHOUGH deity and demon are lavishly presented in the Chinese theatre they do not overbalance the mortal stage types of heroine, ingenue, villain, et cetera, who people the stage of every country.

The ubiquitous human being who conserves his own blood and spills that of his enemy, who weds and repents to solace himself as best he may, who clings to life and dies with valour, is the villain and the hero of Eastern drama as he is the villain and the hero in a Western playhouse. Tradition of doctrine and philosophy and the circumstance of government decorate this universal figure with the trappings of nationality and cause his digression from the general dramatic path to fulfil an occidental or an oriental destiny.

Stage characters in China represent every class of society and are a long list of emperors, generals, scholars, heads of families and sons, and, among

45

women, empresses, court attendants, courtesans, serving women and soldiers, the mother, the wife, the concubine. In associated action, these terrestrial personages appear with gods and not infrequently assume immortal privileges as well as present earthly foible.

Stage characters are classified according to type; and are interesting to an audience as types quite as much as the individuals of the immediate drama in which they may be playing. Each has a traditional makeup that is well known to theatre habitués.

Hsiao Sheng represents young civilians; there are several in each company and they alternate to impersonate hero rôles.

Cheng Sheng appears as an emperor or distinguished person and wears the traditional long and flowing beard.

Wu Sheng impersonates elderly military commanders, and wears a beard.

Tsung Sheng may be a minister of state and must wear a beard.

Wai or Ta Hua Mein has a dark painted face and a villain rôle; Lui Fen also signifies a villain.

Pu Tieh Shik is of martial character and performs feats of strength.

Kung Chiao plays a father or corresponding elderly rôle.

Nan Cho or Pien Eho may be either a clown or deformed person, and has a much painted face.

Wu Chun Hu is a painted-face warrior adept with sword and spear and at tumbling.

Chun Shou Hsia means a soldier's makeup.

Sheng signifies male character and Tan a woman's rôle.

The infrequent appearance of women upon the Chinese stage during the last few centuries has not noticeably affected dramatic presentation except in the amorous parts which, even to an accustomed eye and ear, are sometimes grotesque when mimed by a man. But the youths of eighteen or twenty who are usually seen in feminine rôles are surprisingly natural. They trip about with toes thrust into tiny slippers, to produce the effect of bound feet; their voices are trained to high tones, and their faces are painted in delicate or exaggerated imitation of the infrequent sex. The actors who play feminine rôles receive the highest salaries. As in the early Greek and Roman dramas women's rôles are sometimes played by eunuchs.

The following list includes the important feminine rôles.

Cheng Tan, an empress or principal wife.

Hua Tan, who takes youthful rôles and may be the heroine.

Hsiao Tan, the house servant type who may be an intermediary in social intrigue.

Wu Tan, who impersonates a woman soldier, and of whom there may be four in a company.

Wen Wu Tan assumes either military or civil character and may be the heroine.

Chan Tan is a young married woman. He usually has considerable ability as a singer.

Fu or Lao Tan represents elderly women.

Nu Chou signifies a wicked and disagreeable person.

Tang Tan represents several minor characters.

Ma Tan is a serving woman or soldier.[1]

The majority of these rôles require a painted face; and colours symbolize types. A sly but dignified person paints with white; a sacred person, either a deity or an emperor, uses red colouring; black belongs to the honest workman; green sometimes means a demon; and gold is the property of the gods. Variations on these definite types may be suggested by mixed colours.

On the program the characters are announced as well as the names of the actors. The entrance of an important player is, at times, followed by a self introduction in which he talks of the person he is to

[1] Characters quoted from W. Stanton's book, "The Chinese Drama"; with one or two added from information received from Mr. Shen Hung, a Chinese actor.

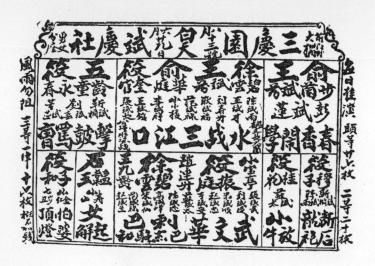

PROGRAM OF A THEATRE IN PEKING, 1920,
ON WHICH EIGHT PLAYS ARE ANNOUNCED

present; sometimes he will recount in detail his family history, why he appears, where he is from, and what he desires to accomplish during the entire period of the play; he may even repeat certain of these speeches upon a second and a third entrance —these repetitions of character exposition are often erroneously omitted in translated plays.

Throughout a performance an intimate relation is maintained between the characters and the audience.

# VI

# *The Actors*

"The art of the actor cuts the sinews
of all earnest government."

THE Chinese actor seldom experiences in private life any of the respect that his rôles obtain within the theatre. An occasional re-
markably gifted player attached to a permanent
theatre in Peking or Canton—and who makes a good
deal of money—may end by receiving superlative
defence but he is the rare exception in his profession. A Mei Lan-fang.

Usually deriving from low birth, and inheriting the
position of a social outcast which developed for
actors during the Mongol dynasty, he is cut off from
other society than that of theatre people. Until recently the descendants of an actor, to the third generation, were forbidden to compete in the public
examinations which offer to the poor man in China
the unique opportunity to acquire wealth and influence.

The manager of a travelling troupe of players not

infrequently buys very young boys and trains them to become members of his company. During six years each is forced to learn innumerable plays and their accompanying songs; to become enough of an athlete to perform the acrobatic tricks which are so popular a part of military plays; to walk with bound feet in case he develops an ability to take women's rôles; and to exercise an hour a day with head thrown back and mouth stretched wide to strengthen his voice. All of this time he is under the implacable rule of a master, and his diet is fixed and frugal. To better this condition to any extent in later years an actor must display a marked talent or meet and please an influential patron of the stage who will purchase his independence.

Sons of actors have few opportunities to enter any other profession than that of the theatre.

There is no prompter, and every player must memorize from one to two hundred rôles. He must also cultivate the quality of suggestion for, by the inflection of his voice, by action and gesture, it devolves upon him to suggest absent properties and scenery.

Actors are often hired by wealthy men to provide an evening's entertainment in a private house. When the guests sit down to dinner five players in rich costume enter and bow profoundly. One of them presents a book in which the titles of several scores of plays are written. The list is examined by the principal guests and if the name of any one of them is found among the names of the characters in a play the piece containing it is immediately discarded from the possible ones chosen for presentation. Etiquette is so crystallized and carefully maintained in China that even such slight association with an actor is against social tradition.

Mei Lan-fang is an exception to this national prejudice against the actor, and his popularity promises to bring about a change in the Chinese attitude towards all actors. He is called China's foremost actor. He is certainly its most liked. When one has seen him play this is easily understood for his art is superb and appealing. To watch him act is to realize how rarely we see this common art perfected. Although he has made experiments with a Western type of play production his present interest is entirely in old drama. His repertory includes several hundred plays. Of these many have been restored, through Mr. Mei's study of the exacting drama tradition, to their original unity of dance and song and pantomime. His art is so admired that his songs have frequently been rewritten for him by China's foremost poets.

Mei Lan-fang plays only feminine parts. The use

of his hands, his glance, his voice, the poise of his body, his harmony of rhythm, are wholly feminine. He is slight, his hands and face are sensitively modelled and never inactive, and his accurate body holds that secret of rhythm which so few dancers possess, unarrested movement.

It is frequently said that there have been no actresses in China, but during the Mongol and the beginning of the Ming dynasty women took all feminine rôles. The Ming emperor Ch'ien Lung forbade their appearance upon the stage for the reason that his mother had been an actress—it was during the thirteenth century that a law was passed ranking actresses and courtesans in the same official group. From that time until towards the finish of the Manchu power in 1911 actresses were seldom seen. The profession was considered to offer individual privilege and a freedom from moral restraint that has periodically been frowned upon by a nation in which the majority of women are still at the disposal of fathers and husbands.

It is the "courtesanes savantes" who, in some measure, have continued the feminine element in the theatre during the prohibitive years. They have been playwrights, and are often portrayed as stage characters—they should not be confounded with the "women who smile in public" who are seldom presented upon the stage. These "courtesanes sa-vantes" attend and understand the theatre and may become actresses; they belong to an established order of educated women and must qualify in many stud-ies before they are "diplomée." Each possesses what seems to be all the charms of spirit as well as of per-son. . . . "In order that a young girl be admitted into the society of courtesans . . . it is necessary that she is distinguished by beauty, by the delicate perceptions of her spirit, and a careful education; she must understand vocal music, the flute, the gui-tar, the dance, history and philosophy; she must also be able to write all the characters of 'Tao-té king'—a book which contains the doctrines of the philosopher Lao-tsu and is one of the most obscure volumes in the Chinese language. When she has spent several months in the Pavilion of One Hundred Flowers; when she knows how to dance and sing and play a castanette accompaniment she becomes a 'free' woman; she then feels above the young girl who is dependent upon her father or the legal con-cubine who is under the protection of her husband, and above the widow who is dependent upon her son"; [1] but while her "freedom" excuses her from duties peculiar to her sex it debars her from civil and religious ceremonies.

[1] M. Bazin in "Théatre Chinois."

MEI LAN-FANG KILLING THE GENERAL IN "THE BANDIT GENERAL"

Today the actress is again commonly seen in China and is usually histrionically gifted. In Peking women sometimes maintain their own theatres and appear with men or form separate companies of their own sex and play men's rôles.

There are many classes of male actors: the first in importance is the permanent theatre group who appear only in a few large cities; temporary players perform in temples in cities and villages; the Ts'au Dan Shi or Grass Stage Players also perform in villages but build a stage upon the grass; the Kang Woo Pei or River and Canal actors who live upon boats, use this floating domicile as a stage and are content with an audience that gathers upon the river bank. There is a great army of solitary players—the Speaking Books—these men appear in tea houses and restaurants; their accomplishments are singing and story telling.

The itinerant actor group includes the frequently met master of a trick monkey; the strolling musicians with a drum and gong to sound and a few stories to relate; and the men who are heard upon bridges and street corners chanting historical fact and adventure. These solitudinarians, who are particularly ill paid, ill treated beyond their fellows, and as despised as human beings may be, have not even the companionship of their own kind to mitigate their sad existence; they earn only a sufficient number of cash [1] each day to buy the two bowls of rice which maintains their strength to wander.

In Peking there are many permanent theatres and a pronounced interest in the drama, and actors like to consider themselves native of this city no matter how far outside its gates they may be forced to travel. There, where the most talented may live the year round in quarters in the theatre district, maturity occasionally brings one of them the lenitive of success—as in the case of Mei Lan-fang—but to the majority, either permanently placed or among the ambulant entertainers of the nation, whatever comedy and content the actor may experience is within the illusory existence of the playhouse itself.

[1] A cash is considerably less than an American penny.

# VII

# *The Music*

"The former kings ordained music
to inspire reverence for virtue."

T O unaccustomed ears the music in Chinese
theatres—usually played fortissimo and with
much brass—is as formless and lacking in
melody as sound may be. It is an art developed for
Chinese people and is based upon a different scale
from the one the Western auricular sense has been
trained to register with pleasure. Before we consider
the importance of music in the theatre it is well to
understand something of the principles which govern
Chinese musical sound.

Music is a measurable art. With the realization that
tone measurement varies in different parts of the
world one begins to understand why the Occidental
may not respond with pleasure to Chinese music.
The Western scale is tempered, and because we are
trained to the almost imperceptible deviation from
the absolute purity of its intervals the nerves of the
ear cannot endure, without offense, the excess or

59

deficiency in an interval of the Chinese untempered scale. And while the Chinese have what corresponds to our chromatic scale, tone measurement is not the same.

In China a scale of five tones was in general use until B. C. 1100, when two more tones were added by the system of measuring sound with lüs-bamboo reeds. The scale became like the Western diatonic and was composed of five full tones and two half tones, but one of the latter occurred between the fourth and fifth degrees instead of in its Western place between the third and fourth degrees.

When the Mongol warrior Kublai Khan became emperor he introduced a new scale of ten notes; during the Ming dynasty this was rearranged: all notes producing half tones were excluded and the scale became pentonic again; but while it contained only seven notes it measured more than an octave.

Such experiment and change unite to increase the difficulties of Chinese music in its own country as well as in the West and add to Occidental prejudice.

"According to Chinese ideas music rests upon two fundamental principles—the shên-li or spiritual, immaterial principle, and the ch'i-shu or substantial form. All natural productions are represented by unity; all that requires perfecting at the hands of man is called under the generic term (wan), plurality.

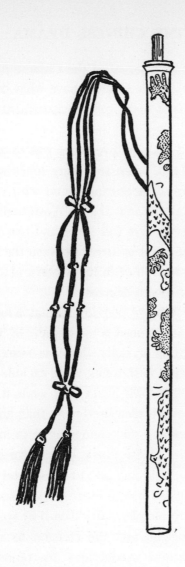

BAMBOO

Unity is above, it is heaven; plurality is below, it is earth. The immaterial principle is above, that is, it is inherent in material bodies, and is considered their (pên) basic origin. The material principle is below; it is the (shing) form or figure of the shên-li. The form is limited to its proper shape by (shu) number, and it is subjected to the rule of the shên-li. Therefore when the material principle of music (that is, the instruments) is clearly and rightly illustrated, the corresponding spiritual principle (that is, the essence, the sounds of music) become perfectly manifest." [1]

The Chinese have always liked to find a similitude of contrast existing between everything in creation. Between heaven and earth, they say, there is perfect harmony. Three is the emblem of heaven and two the symbol of earth. If two sounds arc in the proportion of three to two they will harmonize as perfectly as heaven and earth.

"On this principle the Chinese evolved musical sound through a series of bamboo tubes differing in length; the first tube was cut nine inches long, and the second exactly two-thirds this length, which rendered a perfect fifth—in European music also expressed by a ratio of three to two. The second bamboo, being treated on the same principle, produced

[1] J. A. Van aalst.

a third tube measuring exactly two-thirds of the length, and giving a note a perfect fifth higher than that of the second tube. This new sound seeming too far distant from the first or fundamental note, the length of the producing tube was doubled and the note became an octave lower." [1] The tubes engendered one another and always measured two-thirds or four-thirds of their generator. These bamboo tubes are known as lüs.

This short technical account may serve to show that Chinese music is not merely the "delirious noise" the Westerner is apt to style it and then dismiss from his mind as something without principle or value. And when we realize that the eight men (Pang-Mein) who form the orchestra must serve a long apprentice to learn the technique of moon-guitars, flute, two-string fiddle, cymbals, drums, and gongs which make up the theatre orchestra, we are further convinced that there are directions and difficulties for the Oriental musician which are quite as exacting as those for the European.

In theatres the orchestra is usually seated at the back of the stage. The man who plays the side drum is the conductor—when such a person is needed,—he is known as the Ku Shou. The Shang Shou plays the moon-guitar, flute, and reeds; San Shou plays cym-

[1] J. A. Van aalst.

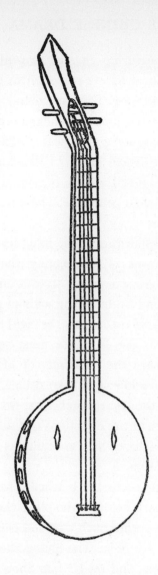

YUE K'IN
GUITAR WITH FOUR CORDS IN SILK OR METAL,
PLAYED WITH FINGER NAIL OR SMALL PICK

bals and the two-string violin which is so popular an instrument among celestial music lovers; it varies in form but never has more than two strings. They are tuned to a distance of a fifth from each other. The Erh Shou plays the three-string violin, reeds and flute. Other men play upon large and small metal or stone gongs and various drums; and there is a player to relieve with the brasses.

Each style of music is named. To illustrate: Erh-Wang is played during solemn, and Pang tsu during martial, action. Every musical theme has its particular emotional appeal and its significance is understood by the audience. A few characters in a play may have an associated melody as in Occidental musico-dramatic performance.

A change in the music is indicative of a change in the action, and announces an attendant event—a battle, a marriage, a burial. Stringed instruments usually accompany singing; but drums, cymbals, gongs, and castanets may sound in the finale. In listening to Chinese music the strike of a wooden stick upon a block, by which the conductor marks time, is agreeably evident.

During military plays, strings, in conjunction with the drums and cymbals of Western martial association, replace the wind instruments. After a quotation or a command spoken by an actor cymbals sound ten or fifteen notes in rapid succession, and often drown his voice—but as the audience has usually seen the play, or another almost identical, so many times that it knows what he is saying, this conflict of sound is not considered to matter. Cymbals also provide the only evident separation between the several dramas on each day's program, which, with only such musical warning, follow in quick sequence.

Chinese musical instruments have been made from stone, earth, metal, bamboo, wood, silk, skin, and gourds, and each material has its traditional association with nature.

History guarantees the existence of music in China as far back as the forty-fifth century before Christ when it attributes the seven-string lute to Fou-hi. And the ardent editor Confucius wrote of music that was played in B. C. 2200; and mentioned that it was passing through a decadent period during his own lifetime.

About the tenth century A. D., during the second era of drama significance, a singing rôle which has continued to the present time, was introduced into plays to accompany and elaborate the speaking part. In the earliest translated Chinese plays the words of these songs were often omitted as they were supposed to be of slight importance; actually they are necessary for sequence and emphasis, and contain much of the poetry and delicate sentiment of the play.

Musical themes are traditional in the theatre and are constantly repeated to accompany new groupings of words. The songs interest an audience less as composition than for the manner in which they are sung. They are often long recitatives in which words are pronounced to several successive notes, and differ from the sacred music of China, which is slow and sweet, in that the songs of the theatre are sung in high and shrill head tones, or falsetto.

They differ in significance from the Greek chorus, and are sung by one person who is usually the principal character, and who may be drawn from any social condition. In the "Sorrows of Han" the singer is an emperor; in the "Intrigues of a Maid" it is a young slave girl. In this use of the singing among the spoken rôles a theory of dramatics offered by Lopé de Vega was illustrated long before he lived. De Vega said that when a man wishes to give counsel he speaks in a different tone with a studied choice of words and an emphasis that he would not use in ordinary conversation.

Musical notation in China is difficult to understand both because it varies in old and new music and because it is inexact. The native musicians say that to be able to decipher manuscript music they must first hear it played. A sheet of music looks very much like a page of writing to the foreigner, who can read neither, as no staff is used in music; and notes, after the manner of ideographs, are printed from the top of the page down and from right to left. The tone symbols have changed with the succeeding dynasties: there are twelve in present usage. They may be written in two sizes to suggest two octaves, and dots are sometimes added to indicate held notes, two for a half and three for a whole note. The usual time is four-four, although three-four tempo is also popular. Space left between two notes may indicate a rest, but the time duration must either be learned or be decided by individual pleasure. When words are printed with music they are placed between the notes.

However irregular notation may be the origin of music is authentic and ancient; and the sound of it in the theatre, either sung by young actors or played upon strings and reeds and metal, is of remarkable emotional significance and appeal. Although a dissimilar sense perception renders Chinese music unpleasant to the average Westerner, an occasional Occidental agrees with the Chinese to find it passionate, provocative, submissive, commanding, or sentimental, in accord with the action of the play, and of an inherent and singular beauty.

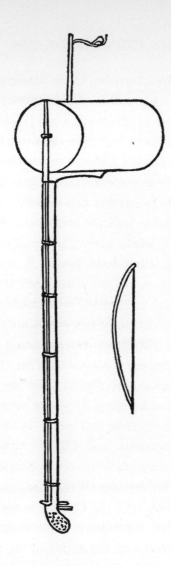

HOU K'IN OR TWO-STRING VIOLIN

MEI LAN-FANG IN A SWORD DANCE

# VIII

# *Decoration, Costume, and Symbolic Design*

**D**ECORATION is usually considered as an external of the drama. In China, however, it has so profoundly filtered into the dramatic spectacle through the national disposition to symbolism (in all the seductive fantasie of form and colour to which the symbol lends itself) that decoration has become an essential, as well as a sentient, component of the classical theatre. And this occurs in a country where the stage has no scenery. Such apparent anachronism is explained by Chinese that as their theatre is not imitative, landscape, or an interior, is created for an audience by suggestion; by emotion; and, it must be confessed of the theatre habitué of today, by drama tradition.

To the Chinese, scenery is a "silly and unnecessary bother." A court event which may have taken place centuries ago in a magnificent entourage will be reproduced in the playhouse with every detail of costume and mode of speech carefully exact but without scenery and with almost no stage furnishing. The imagination that has created in Chinese art so much chimerical humour of animal and flower and fetish can find a river where there is no water, and a mountain where none is painted.

Prescribed action creates scenery! If some character must climb a mountain, pantomimic motions assume the presence of the granite hill. If a criminal is to be executed it is accomplished with a bamboo pole and traditional movements on the part of the actor. He, the criminal, wails a confession of guilt, walks to one side of the stage and stands under a bamboo pole on which a cloth is tied; he indicates strangulation by throwing back his head and looking up to heaven. If, in a stage story, a general goes upon a journey, the scene is not changed to transport one's mind to another place, instead the soldier cracks a whip, dashes across the stage to a crash of cymbals, and announces that he has arrived. To dismount from his absent steed he pirouettes upon one foot and drops his whip; to mount he turns upon the other foot and picks up his whip. If a plot demands that a fairy enter in a chariot of clouds, a feminine figure advances bearing horizontally two flags upon which clouds and wheels are painted; she is accompanied by another actor in the ubiquitous blue cotton of the Chinese workman.

Upon the stage a man may drink wine in which, unknown to himself, a venomous snake has been dissolved, he may suffer a frightful irritation, throw himself into a pond, wash, and find himself cured, in a propertyless pantomime that is perfectly understood by his audience. Rivers, walls, temples, groves, thrones, couches, are represented by a bench or screen, and if the acting is good everyone is satisfied.

But if scenery exists only in the imagination, costumery is splendidly authentic and is frequently of astonishing beauty. Chinese costume—like plumcake —from the very richness of its material, is long lived; and the clothes used in today's theatre may have been worn several centuries ago by mandarins and court officials, by emperors, their wives and concubines.

As Chinese dress was designed for ceremonial purpose—a cloak in which to hide any condition of spiritual or physical poverty—and to present men to the world as they wished to appear, it is not difficult to realize why it is so magnificent and costly. The traditional stage dress of even a beggar is a silk coat of a gay checked design. There is a tradition too to be followed in the "barbarian's" dress, and he must wear a bit of fur about his throat no matter what the temperature.

The necessity for accuracy in stage dress means
that an actor's wardrobe may be so expensive that
he more often hires than owns it. Establishments
exist to furnish stage clothes by the season to an
entire company; and servants, who return every costume to its particular box after each wearing, are
included in the rental price.

Faces are painted with red, black, white, green,
and gold, and add their colour characterization to
the spectacle. The effect, even without scenery, that
is obtained by groups of painted figures dressed in
stiff brocade of all tints, by the glitter of immense
jewels, of gold traceries and silver tissue, of tufted
plumes and long pheasant feathers that wave above
glistening headdresses, of glinting swords and bril-
liantly uniformed soldiery, is of memorable dazzle
and magnificence.

Pierre Loti mentions [1] the stage trappings for the
actors who played in the Empress' theatre in Peking,
and which he was privileged to see when he was one
of the Occidental soldiery appointed to guard the
looted Imperial City in which the imperial ruler,
Tsŭ-Hsi, gratified her whims and cruelties, her emotional desires and her demand for entertainment, during the years she lived behind the inner walls of
Peking. Tsŭ-Hsi was deeply entertained by the the-

[1] "The Last Days of Pekin."

"Age"

Symbol for "Happiness"

TWO COMMON CHINESE SYMBOLS

atre and wrote a few plays herself for palace presentation.

Loti says: "I arrive in time to see . . . the decorations, emblems, and accessories of the Chinese Imperial theatre. They were cumbersome, frail things, intended to serve but for a night or two, and then forgotten for an indefinite time in a room which was never opened . . . mythological representations were evidently given at this theatre, the scene taking place either in hell or with the gods in the clouds; and such a collection as there was of monsters, chimeras, wild beasts and devils, in cardboard or paper mounted or carcasses made of bamboo or whalebone, all devised with perfect genius for the horrible, with an imagination surpassing the limits of a nightmare."

It is this imagination surpassing a nightmare that shaped avatar and devil to scurry and swoop as stage character, and that wove grotesque and fantastic forms into brocaded robe for Mongol and Ming and Manchu to reappear upon the stage of today. Although fact and fancy offer rare latitude for spectacular effect they maintain this separation: gods and mortals as stage people may be creatures of imagination, or legendary portraits—if a god has made the step from person to personification—but costumes must be either authentic or minutely copied from models of the period they dress.

Candles, lamps, or, in a few permanent theatres, electric lights, illumine the stage, but lighting for artistic purpose is not included in the Chinese theory of dramatic art.

The Chinese differ from many other Eastern people in that they understand the ancient symbols woven or painted or cut into their decoration and continue to utilize them to tell a story or reflect an early superstition—to protect, to ridicule, to praise.

Tae-Keih, or Great Monad, is a significant symbol in Celestial design. It represents the dualistic principle of man and woman (the male in the female and the female in the male); and the harmony of the universe is supposed to depend upon the balance maintained between these two elements. This design is everywhere, on book, wall, porcelain, tablet, and brocade. It is a symbol of Chinese cosmogony. It may apply to opposites that exist in pairs—to the world and hades, to the sun and moon, to hard and soft. The great Monad symbolizes the basis of Chinese philosophy, science, and religion, and thus its universality in decoration is inevitable.

In China the dragon is the male element. He is the emblem of Heaven as, since B. C. 206, he has been the device of emperors. He is a stage character and appears in apparent flesh as well as in sinuous embroidery. Although he is wingless he has the power

MEI LAN-FANG IN "THE SUSPECTED SLIPPER"

to rise in the air at will. As the sender of rains and floods and the ruler of the clouds he dominates the type of village stage performance which is arranged during a too rainy season to pray for dry weather. The earth dragon marks the course of rivers.

The monkey too is immortalized. He is supposed to have existed before there was a Heaven and earth —where we are not informed. He defeated the generals of Heaven in battle and was finally captured by Buddha, in the end to be released from earth wanderings by a mighty traveller.

The fox is a comic symbol whose stage "business" seems limitless. He may be either man or woman, and practises every deceit. His glance is said to be as efficacious as a drop of benzine for removing spots, and soiled garments are left before his shrine.

The god of thunder association is called Lei Shên. His birthday is on the twenty-fourth of the sixth moon, and during the three weeks which precede this date the people feast in his honour. He has three eyes and rides a tiger.

There are many gods in the likeness of men. In the third century the present god of war was a famous general named Kuan Yü. He slept quietly for twelve hundred years until, in 1594, he was deified and became known as Kuan Ti. He is usually in armour and carries a long weapon. Confucians call him the military sage. To the Buddhists he is the god of protection, and to the Taoists the minister of Heaven. In popular usage he is also the head of the military. Although habit is in a great measure responsible for the continuing faith in deity prescience and protection, it is interesting commentary on the popular European legend that China's martial spirit is not awake, to recall that a picture of Kuan Ti hangs in every tent and officer's camp of her million and a half soldiers, and that the god of war is the patron of many trades and professions.

The theatre god is in the likeness of Ming Huang, the eighth century emperor who established a school for actors in the garden of his palace. While most actors have another patron saint to whom they make sacrifice, they are said to pray to the theatre god to be saved from laughing upon the stage. The image of Ming Huang is seen in theatres. The symbol called age represents a force to be placated that is used at birthday celebrations of gods and mortals and finds place upon the stage. For festival use "age" is of carved and gilded wood and is about four feet high; as a motif it decorates many surfaces of porcelain and silk, and its general popularity is a common expression of the psychic effect in associated ideas.

The ideograph for happiness and for bat are both pronounced as "fu" and the Chinese wit often plays

Thunder God

LEI SHEN

with this dual significance in design. If five bats are shown together the five blessings are signified.

There is a group of sacred and profane symbols called the "Hundred antiques" which includes the pearl, a charm against flood and fire; coin, emblem of riches; Artemisia leaf, good fortune; two books, representing learning; and the jade gong which aids in procuring justice.

The "Twelve ornaments" should not be ignored in any consideration of Chinese design; they appear alone or in grouped decoration, and frequently are embroidered upon robes of ceremony worn in the theatre both by actors and the audience. These "Twelve ornaments" are:

1. Sun, in a bank of clouds, with a three-legged bird inside the disc.

2. Moon, containing a hare and a mortar and pestle.

3. Constellation of stars connected by straight lines.

4. Mountains.

5. Five clawed dragon (already mentioned).

6. Flowery fowls, two variegated pheasants.

7. Temple vessels, used in ancestral worship.

8. Aquatic grasses in sprays.

9. Fire in flaming scrolls.

10. Millet grains grouped in medallions.

11. Fu = axe or weapon of warrior.

12. Fu = symbol of distinction or happiness (already mentioned).[1]

Symbols, with confusing frequence, vary in name to accord with the three doctrines of China; they may differ even in form among the Manchus of the north or the Chinese of the south; but however symbol and image may change in outline their presence and influence is universal. Scroll and animal and flower, knots and leaves, claws, scaly tails, fangs and squinting eyes depict fury, malice, cunning, goodness or wisdom; a dragon protects, a fox betrays, a squat old mandarin advises, a bit of golden scroll blesses; monsters of lacquer or bronze or jade; vermilion, nocturnal blue or the yellow of old faïence; deities of the house, the street, the tomb, the temple, the theatre, speak the secrets of the Violet City; and confess in contortions and audacious prostrations the superstitions of the Chinese; to link dynasties and repeat the imponderable fantasie and the bland cruelties of twice two thousand years.

[1] Sir A. W. Franks.

God of War

KUAN TI, A FAMOUS GENERAL IN THE THIRD CENTURY

MEI LAN-FANG

# IX

# Customs of the Playhouse and the Greenroom

THE building in which drama is presented is of little more importance in theatre tradition, and apparently as unnecessary for the enjoyment of a play, as scenery or properties. Only in large cities are permanent theatres to be found.

China is a country of extremes, in wealth and distances as well as in every art expression, and, in spite of its long existence as an amusement for emperors and the wealthy class, the theatre has held to something of the early nomadic habit of the Chinese people who wander—tents more or less under arm—about the country.

The temporary or "mat" theatre made of mats and bamboo poles is the most usual form of playhouse, and one large enough to hold a thousand people may be erected in a few hours from material which each travelling company carries for the purpose.

In town and village a stage may be hastily put up in a field; or a travelling troupe of actors may be allowed to play in a temple or its courtyard if some deity shrined within is featured in the performance. Even a convenient street corner is not disdained by a manager, to whom the actual stage is of small interest.

Superior companies of actors do not travel far from Peking or some other large city where they are less despised and better paid than in small towns, but the majority of troupes are nomadic; and Chinese villages are few which do not have at least one annual series of dramatic performances.

The actor is the troubadour of China. He carries the news, the entertainment, and a degree of instruction to millions of remote people who have no other association with cities than that which is brought to them by the travelling players.

Mat theatres include a stage, a greenroom, several loges in which seats are placed, and, usually, pavilions in which tea and sweets are sold. The majority of the spectators stand or sit upon the ground close to the stage, sometimes remaining a half dozen hours without appearing to tire of the acrobatic tumbling, the grotesque humour, and the military manœuvres that the long performances offer.

Seating arrangements vary with the type of theatre. In a permanent playhouse the stage is at one end with a gallery opposite and loges on either side at the stage level. Both the auditorium and the stage are rectangular. Tables and chairs are in the pit and seats in the rear gallery. Stands for teapots and cups are within reach of everybody, and tea is served continuously; even an actor may be offered a cup of tea while playing, if his part is difficult or prolonged.

All Chinese theatres have certain unhygienic customs such as a common use of wet towels, passed about to "refresh" the audience, the omnipotent teacup, and the unfreshened air, which to an Occidental make the out-of-door performance, even under a hot sun, preferable to the congested audience chamber of the permanent playhouse.

The so-called evil smells of China—in the West China is the proverbial home of the "bad egg"— what they smell of and why they endure, are astounding. They too are traditional; and give pleasure to the Chinese, whose idea of sweet and foul differs from our own, and whose scent perception is so developed that a man sitting within a house is said to know whether or no a passerby is a native of his own town. But to the Westerner who cultivates only his senses of sight and hearing (taste he dulls and touch and smell he scarcely thinks of to secure enjoyment) and who names only a rose or a pudding "sweet" even the mention of Chinese smells is anathema.

The average permanent theatre holds about seven hundred people. A loge is supposed to seat five but no one objects if a few other persons crowd into it. Ideas of comfort in sitting—as in smells—change with the latitude, and the average Chinese is indifferent to what the Occidental calls "comfort."

It is the custom to collect the admission fee during the evening after those persons who may not find themselves interested in the performance have had time to depart. In permanent theatres admission has been no more than twenty-five cents until the last few years when a performance by a celebrated actor may command several times that amount. In temporary theatres entrance is usually free. Country festivals are paid for either by a wealthy man of the village or by popular subscription. Money may be tossed upon the stage at the end of a performance.

Transportation of stage panoply—costumes, mats, et cetera, and the hundred odd people who form the company, is uniquely accomplished. A group of players hires its own "junk" and sails, or is towed, to cities and settlements along the rivers and waterways. The "junk" serves also as hotel, and is one of

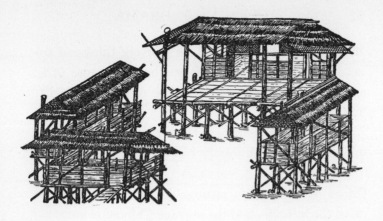

A TEMPORARY THEATRE OF MATS AND BAMBOO

the diverting sights of the heterogeneous river life.

Once a twelvemonth actors disband to form new combinations and sign fresh contracts. Each company is given a name, to which a number may be added, to accord with the rank it holds in the public and in the managerial estimation. Naturally this method is confusing.

The greenroom of a permanent theatre is an exotic spectacle and must be in some degree a confused domicile even to the actor who spends most of his life passing in and out of it, gambling, drinking tea, or sleeping on a pile of boxes, when he is not actually on the stage. Customs, or rather rules, are rigidly enforced in the greenroom; for example: it has always been the privilege of only the actors who impersonate emperors to sit upon the "big clothes box" which belongs to a prominent member of the troupe.

Leading actors have individual dressing rooms, but to the majority of the company the greenroom is both dressing room and property chamber. Make-up stands and tables are frequent and are littered with colours and brushes; and hooks along the walls suspend a medley of masks, false beards, wigs, helmets, thick-soled shoes to increase the stature of their wearers, swords, bows and arrows and early implements of war, symbolic pennants and wands, and the patched and discoloured clothes belonging to the lowest members of the company who take a variety of minor parts and are known as the "waste-paper-basket" players.

Many Chinese actors are pallid and dirty individuals and a great deal of paint is needed to transform them into beautiful women; but there are such exceptions as Mei Lan-fang who are young and comely and who show remarkable skill in makeup. Such men are greatly appreciated upon the stage and when they totter in on their "golden lilies" the audience signifies its approval by calling out "how," meaning good. If a spectator is displeased he is allowed to shout "tung" (bad) and if a sufficient number is dissatisfied with a performance it may be repeated upon demand.

The greenroom is directly behind the stage and equals it in length. Two doors, as entrance and exit, connect them.

The Chinese stage has no curtain to separate the actor and the spectator. A smoke screen is sometimes used to obscure the stage from gods who are being presented upon it and who may be offended to see themselves caricatured or burlesqued.

Such involved and dual use of supernatural characters—impersonation and the concomitant attempt to placate for such imitation, nourishes both the genius and the illusion of a classical drama which in unique artistry has been the paradise of immortal adventurers; the unrolled scroll of grotesque, lascivious, and sacred symbol; and the enriching national picture-book of historic fact and fantasia during the past six centuries of succeeding dynasty and despot, in which a tenacious public has continued a traditional art.